VELKOM TO INKLANDT

First published in the UK in 2017 by Short Books
an imprint of Octopus Publishing Group Ltd
Carmelite House, 50 Victoria Embankment
London, EC4Y 0DZ

www.octopusbooks.co.uk
www.shortbooks.co.uk

An Hachette UK Company
www.hachette.co.uk

This new edition published in 2021

10 9 8 7 6 5 4 3 2 1

A CIP catalogue record for this book is available from the British Library.

ISBN 978-1-78072-534-5

Printed and bound in China

Design by Georgia Vaux

VELKOM TO INKLANDT

POEMS IN MY GRANDMOTHER'S INKLISCH

SOPHIE HERXHEIMER

WITH ORIGINAL PAPERCUTS BY THE AUTHOR

In memory of I.M.H 1902-1980

For ROSA and CONRAD

INKLANDT

London

Not zo mainy Dais zinz ve arrivink.
Zis grey iss like Bearlin, zis same grey Day
ve hef. Zis norzern Vezzer, oont ze demp Street.
A biet off Rain voant hurt, vill help ze Treez
on zis Hempstet Heese ve see in Fekt.
Vy shootd I mind zat?

I try viz ze Busses, Herr Kondooktor eskink
me... for vot? I don't eckzectly remempber;
Fess plees? To him, my Penny I hent ofa –
He notdz viz a keint Smile – *Fanks Luv!*
He sez. Oh! I em his Luff – turns Hentell
on Machine, out kurls a Tikett.

Zis is ven I know zat here to settle iss OK. Zis
City vill be Home, verr eefen on ze Buss is Luff.

Beink Prektikell

Ven you hef to scuttel to ze ferry Etjch; ze Sea –
take viz you two Kitz oont two Grent Muzzers,
like ezz eef you are no bikker zan a skuddink
Claut off Dust, as it flies off ze Brissell off a Broom –

zen yes, of korrs you sharpen efferi Messud off how
to make yourzelf infizziple – you get zo gut at zat,
you ken forkgett enny uzzer Vay – foldink into Korners,
sayink Zilch, becomes ze vun ezzenschel Hebbit.

Ze Raich aghentz zose Maus-foamink, Zeegar-smokink,
sveggerink Sukgz oont Bullee-Boyze is settisfeit –
by plantink, in fresch nors London Urse, efferi
sinkle moddest Sink zat spells: *Ve liff! Ve breez!*

Efferi zin-skintd noddink Frittillery, efferi veksi Kepbej
Rose, each payell Eppel Blossom, iss a Surfivor.

Infentory

Kertense   Vortdropes

    Kuschons

        Lemps oont Lempshates

Divans, Zofas, Betts

        Sowvink Mascheen

    zat Desk

      Armchess

dinink Chess

    ze larch dinink Tapell

        Pots oont Penns

    Zideboart

  Kupboarts

Krokeree   Gremofon Rekorts

  Kutleree

    Books

Ornamentz   Baykink Tinnse

  Piktschers

      Glassvair

Lukkitch

  Klosink   Bootz

      all ze Paypervurk

Mein Gott   Kloks

    Toolse

  Schuze

    Hetts

12

Tektonnik

Ess I vork arount my new City
I sink off you Minna:
are you dedt or alyfe?

I kompose you Lettess in my Hedt:
how to tesskreipe zeze Zmells:
Ze Demp off Ortumm: Roses, Smoke

Olt Kolliflaur, boilt Milk. Streetz hier
are nerrow. Voschink fleps on Leintz;
Efferibotty endlesslee svills Tea.

(Vill you hef a Cup? Oh senk you,
ett no Schukar plees.) Zeze skvot
Rett Brik Howsess hef zmall Vintose,

neat Hedtches oont frunt Gartens,
Bowler-Hetted Chentz et eht
por out, Umprellas kurlt.

Zat svoonink Pienno Musik
zat yusedt to leak in Drifftz from
our Apartment Billtink in Bearlin,

zoffenink it's harsch Korners –
iss nott to be hert, outsite
ze Hummink off it in my Hedt.

In my Hedt: vair you liff olt Frent,
oont vair ve go ofa all of zis:
vair still ve chet oont larf into ze Nyte.

Merritch

He iz tvice ze Sise off a normall Person.
I em harf ze Sise off a normall Person.
Ziss is our ridikuluss Arrainchment.
I'm ze Maus zat cooks oont cleans.
He's ze rorink Elephent who must
reserj ze Intrikusy of ze Bodty
oont ze korekt Medizin to edminister.

He plays on ze Gremofon, zat orvel,
poundink Bruckner.
I serf up my vamous Pork Loin, bekkt
in ze Uffen, viz Unyon.
He plays Chess viz our Zun.
I darn Svetterz viz our Dorter.

Ve velue ze Intellect apuff ze Tittel-Tettel.
He likes to vurk, oont go to bett viz uzzer Vimmin.
I like ze Parks, to voork, oont do ze Garten.
Ze Chiltdren read, do Zums, pass zair Exems.

Who are ve? Ve are chest normall Peepl.
Two off ze Pork eating Choos off olt Inklant.

My Demesk Tapell-Kloss

Vis efferi Snip off Dill I fezzer
on my feinly slizzered Kewkumpers
I re-azzempel Leipzig:
its eleghent Promenaats!

Vis efferi chop off peelt Eppel
es it suds into my Disch for Pie –
I know vair I em!
Etchvair – ortinerry, I kerry on.

Vis efferi Kepbej zat I schret
into my Kepbej Zoop I zummon
up ze Ghostz off zose
who did not stendt a Charntz.

Ven I votch ze Ekks, hard
boilink, bobbink, in ze scheiny Pen –
his Hedt, my Hedt – I'm gledt
he goes avay. Veederzehn!

Ven ze Chilltdren fill ze dottetd Bolse
viz Raspberrees in ze Garten,
sprinkell zem viz Schukar,
eat zem up – I'm zen kontennt.

Vis efferi Zip of Brendy,
efferi puff off *Player's Gold*
I raice in secret to my Lipz,
I holdt out for Opblifion.

Off Eppels Ve Neffer Tire

Zay hurtel off ze Tree
ze Vindt duzzent simpasize
vizz zair Broosink.

I keep ze Box Room kool,
saif upp ze purple indenttett
Cartborts zat kraidell

eetch sleepy Froot Vun by Vun
in zeparett Betts, zat vay
zay stay goot, unrottett

by proximity to anuzzers'
meggoty Vurminks or Dekay!
Zay suztain us viz zair solitt

Flesch, zair Effinitee viz Speiss
ze Chellee of zair Kores ven boilt
ze Eenozentz of zair Blossom.

Alvays zo velkom: in Leipzig,
Tashkent, Vestvoord Ho!
Zay're klose Femmily, vide-zpretd.

Bitz oont Bopse

<u>Grosseriese:</u>
Karrottz, Gherkinz, Kepbej
Peese (in Podts!) Cherzee Royellse,
Harv a Tuzzen Ekks,
a Harv Pount off Chetdar,
Tomato Puray,
Schukar Lumpse,
Finnikar, Musstart

<u>Bootschers:</u>
a Pount best Mintz
oont Harf Pount off Tungk

<u>Hepperdesscherz:</u>
Sretd, oont fife Yarts off Closs for ze new Kertense,
Pinse oont Neetells, Vendty two ply,
Ettrektif Buttonse

Ze Khemist

Mutti's Preskrippschon

Kolt Kriem, Esperin,

Senniterry Nepkinz

Box off zat nize Yartley's Leffenter Zope

Blue Grarse Barse Zaltz (Greta.)

Laibree

Return Amelia Bedelia oont Chekhov

Kollekt ze Schairlock Holmz for Franz.

Arkate Staschonerz

a Burseday Kart for Greta:18!

Airmayell Ennfelopes

Blue-bleck Ink —

Allyze

Ve are zo korllt Aliensse,
and zat makes makink
Frentz zeem, if not
impossipel: empischus!

I'fe been zo gled zen,
diskoffrink Upstezz Muriel –
she vonts Nussink more
zan to bump into me!

Ve all ettmayer her zilky
Hayr oont her Kleffernesse,
she eefen hess en interestink
Chob in Veithall: she's

a sifill Serfent. She first nokt
ven ze Aroma off Kerravay
in my Kesserole voftett to her
Noztrills in ze Flett apuff.

She introtrewst herzelf,
ve mett alzo her Husspent.
(A dull Menn I'm afrait. Viz
uss she takes Refuche!)

She kiffs me Beckgrount
Kloose about ze Nayporhoodt,
oont Inklisch Vayze. Ve tork
of interneschionell Affezz.

Ve share ze Reschens:
a schort Kaffee, my not-zo-sveet
Strudel. How ve larf togezzer
ven on ze Auer, Mrs Finton,

ze Vooman next Tor,
flyse into her Yart, oont kryse
out in metd Inraichment:
Go avay – you blutty Forennas!

Ze Mornink off a Haus-Vyfe, Vair to Beghin

Putt ze gezzert Lefft-ofas in Tuppavairs?
Shake from ziss Kloss its klingink
Krumps off Toste? Make Jemm
from all zeze Vint-Fall Garten Plumpz?

Zis Floor kryse out for a Moppink.
Ze Sink iss krayvink Bleech.
Ze Ziteboart neetds a Beeze-Veks Pollisch
Zair is a larch demp Vosch to Peg out.

Bah! I vill instet to ze Laibree march.
Ziss Mess iss OK unkontemplaytett for
en Auer! I vill zurch a Book, Somesink
viz real Filss: Murter oont Low Leif!

Ven I return, I'll grientd ze scheiny Beense —
make myself a *Kitschin Durt Kaffee* —
allow myself vun Chepter — maybe Sefferell.
Ze konzentratett Ztreem of kontinentell

Bitterness vakes oont lulls in eekvel Messchur —
Nofell, Koffee, Zigarette — lifts zat
punkschuate Monotony, before I vunse
akhen opbleich ziss neghink Haus I vedtet!

Sowvink Mascheen

Leik a Drekgon in en olt
Book – Blek oont Golt.
He hess a Tredtle,
zo it's eesy to go
vizzink alonk ze Kloss.

Vhrr Vhrr Vhrr. He singks
in hiz own Lenkvitch.
Togezzer ve get lost
in ze Kvest to make Efferisink
look ess krisp es Drekgons

oont zair Mountenz!
Ve kuschon vot iss hart,
oont feschon ze ingulfink
Shertz from ze Outfitterz
into trim Blauziz.

His scharp Toose snares,
oont his silfer Fut stempz
impekabel Highvayse
of Stitchiss zet desch akross
ze flettent Kotten Lawn.

Ve make Ennysink:
Leffenter Beks to Eefenink Vair
to petsch-pokketitt Pycharmers.
Goot Drekgon – safes zis
Vooman from beink

eaten alyfe by Pointlessnesse.
Frees her into a mejjick Lentd
off Pettenz, Pinkink Scheerz,
oont Sylko. Holtz her Tenschon
viz his fiery Sredt.

A Dorter Also

She neffer zdops viz
her sharp-Eit Opservaschonz:
Liesel! Vot is zat Enfelope in ze Hall?
Hef you en Edmirer, eefen hier in Inklandt?

Her Spektakells are like great see-sru
Pepbles, oont her Cloze, infareeaplee
in ze Vittow's blek, releevt vrom Gloom
(vitch by ze Vay she duss not zuffer from)
by tiny veit Dottz or uzzer such small
Petterns in zimpel Roller-print Repeatz.
Her svollen Feet rest in zair vide blek Schuze,
like Ghengster's Spetts. Her veit lonk Hair,
iss efferi Day tvistit into ze low-down Bun.
Vot an olt Owl she iz.

To ze Kitz, she zeems zo sveet, zo harmlesse –
ze kvintissenschal kontinentel olt Lady – viz ziss
Guinee-Vowl Get-up, oont ze Vorkink-Stick: tep, tep.
But to me – she iz foreffer my fee-urse Muzzer –
her beadty Eye kept traint on me:
Liesel! Vair are you goink?
Muzzer! I'm sixty-seffn, oont I don't hef to tell you!
Zen, ze Perz-Lipt Porze; ze Kvestion hengink:
alvays I kan't help to Kayfe in.
Yes; vell. I'm goink to ze Laibree.

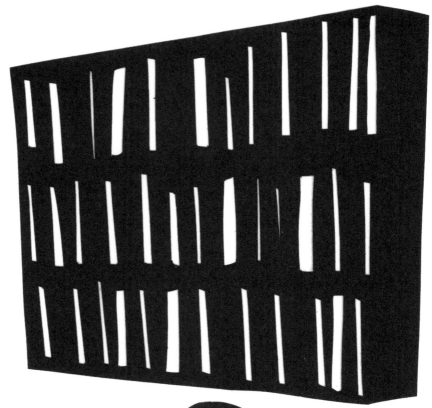

Ze Print in Ze Hall

Ven leafink or enterink
ze Haus, allvays
I get Strenks from
a Glarntz et ze Print
zat henks by ze Door.

Littel Greta telse me
zat she duzzent leik it.
Ze Grey, ze Veit oont ze Blek...
zoze are my vurst, most borink Kullors —
togezzer viz zis drippy Yellow,
not eefen a nice brite Yellow,
she size, viz a Keint
off exasperaitett Dizpair.

I larff, she is funny viss ziss
Mindink off how Efferisink looks.
I leik zis Pikscher, I say her.
Ze Grey, ze Veit oont ze Blek
seem peeseful to me, zay
take ze Fluster out off zis
orvel Leafink oont Kummink bek:
nice trenkvill Shates.

I know zat she stares oont
stares at ziss Piktscher,
hess a Fessinayschon
viz it in Fekt.

Ze Sink zat ve bose re-ektink
to iss ze Zubjekt Metter: Nunns!
Grefick in zair Vayells,
ebstrected in zair shedowt Kloyster.

Zay svay allonk zo graisefull, oont
to me, zay look zo free, but to her
zay look treppt in zat Place,
oont in ze terribel Kullor Skeem
off her Skool Uniform.

Renaysonz via Norzern Lein

I bortd from Etchvair ett Noon
meet him by ze Botticelli
Mars oont Venus vizzin ze Auer.

Brontse oont green Cheks
are karpetink ze Zeats, oont
for readink: Simenon's *Maigret*.

Cherrink Kross: et Rist-Votch glarntz,
ekxit. Ziz same Lein from Tootink
he hess kort, zat's vair he liffs

viz Titian, his Kett. He vayfes
his Hentz in frunt off Rafaell
oont zoze Itellians, his Veekness

opfius for zoft Metdonnas.
For me ze Cranachs vin Hentdz down.
Vy? Bekoss ze Truse iss neffer

zimpel Bewtee! Ve leik diskussink
Metters zat take uss kvite far from
ze dull off Efferiday. Ve treffell alonk

shairtd rusty Trecks, ettempt
Moufment in lonk helt Oppinnyonz,
vell... Ideas don't martch in Leintz!

Zey svurl about leik Plooms off Kullor,
make unekspektett Stopz!
Kvestyuns breetd Unsertennty:

Vot a Vreedom! Zis suztains me
on ze homevootd Train — vair I'm releeft
to reet ze tyte-upp Entink off my Book.

Dess Bett

Laik a Birt Skelitin in ze Hospitell Neit-Gown
I'm harf-vay to Dust. In zis kletterink,
bedt-Food smellink Voord, I'm Etchvair kvy-et.
tuckt in a Prayree off veit Sheetz.

A plompisch Girl enters, rarzer vyalt,
her flountzy Dress makes a Dent in ze klinikel
Husch, my Vissiter! She plonks herselff
boomp on ze Bett, turnss her smutchy

madte-up Featschurs tovoord me. Heffy oont puffy
viz kerryink Sednesse (es vell es Books!) she blurts
awfull Nuse: ze Sueysite off a Frent. (Zum Frent —
to do a tretfull Sink like zat!) Zayventeen also.

But — vy? I esk. *Fet up, I suppoze,* she tries.
But fet up? Zlowly my Stick-sinn Arms
I raice, high up each Seit off my Face.
I tell her: *I hef been fet up too, up to here!*

She kaises et me, Eisse brimmink: I must
look zo terripbel, I'm kvite schriffellt!
Ve all luff you zo much you know — she sess,
Bah! I menedge a Snort, not bekaus I don't

beeleef her, but Luff's a Sink ve neffer
menschen. Ve bose know zis Rule, chest
es ve bose know ze rottett Stomek off Dizpair.
Ziss iss vot makes us...   indeeztruktibel.

CHERMENNY

Kortschipp Valtz

Zay go on all ze uschuell Sinks:
Intellichentz! Vells, Klars oont zoschell
Ztendink, (Chooischnesse? Nein? Ja!)

Vot are ze Fekts? Ask zis apuff Efferisink.
Ve are all esspowst to Sy-entz oont
in Luff viz apuff all, ze Reschonell.

Still a Darntz iz Somesink to look
forvart to. I em fittet viz en ekstettik Tress:
veit, aksentett viz a Zilken Sesch in Blue.

Ve Girls kerry each a Paper Fenn.
On it ve ghezzer Zignetturs: yunk
Menn who visch viz uss to darntz.

I votch, ess he inscreips in Blek:
Max Zimmerspitz – a Flurisch off
Penmenschip – zo zimpel – viz vun

pleasink Inklinaschon off my Hedt
he hess me foreffer tezzert to his Rissm,
his Tune. Hiss Hokkey Keptenn's Bulk,

tvurls me from zat Day to ziss — hiss Feet
ett ze base of Dekkaytes off Snores oont
Pycharmas, off impaschent Streits

arount larch Apartments, tryflink Housiss.
He lurches me, Doll-leik, ofa ze polischt
Parkay off Merritch, Leipzig to Bearlin to

Etchvair, vair still ve notd to Lochik. Eesy
to ent up viz Somevun hartlesse, ven you
vurschip only ze Fekts. But zen, zo much vurs

koot it hef been, vizzout my scharp Nose
for Re-ellity. It'z my Grip on zis, not hiss,
zat brinks us out of zis Valtz alyfe.

Klaus' Furrs

My Farzer's Ensuzee-esm
for Kemistry, oont Zuksess —
leets him to infent new Vays to dye
ze Enimal Furrs — all ze voguisch
Raich zay zoon becomink.

Regard ze Ladies of Leipzig;
zen ze entire Kontinent,
svoddellt in lookschuriuss
Pialls off Lilekk Mink, Mint
Rebbit, Arktik Foks in Rose.

Svelte Figurs sashayink
to zis or zat Soirée. Ze chic
Cleek off Heels, ze Fizz,
ze Cleenk off Chooellree
on ze Schempain Coupes.

Ze Furr Fectory iz a-virr viz
nofellty Kollars, Stollz, zoft Peltz
to sooze, oont melt eefen
ze kolltest, ritchest Hartz,
oont lend zair Show ov Voormz.

Ven Klaus false ill viz Kenser,
viz bik Ideas his Eis still schein —
he vispers uss: *Et Least
enkaich a Strink Kvortett
for my approachink Funerell.*

His Korpse lies kullorless,
his Veks Moustache oont sin
Smile intekt – edrift in Dess –
oont ze Voft off fadett Palms
oont hefty Pearfumes.

Two Veeolins (like my Tvinn
Bruzzers) a Veeola (for me)
ze Chaylo (Mutti) billow Kullor.
From efferi ake-ink, sveepink Strink:
ritsch Huse svell oont rise,

fillink efferi Ear oont Hart
off ze Soules kollekted,
viz Life oont ritch Infentschon:
Zmoke-Blue, Karmeen, Golt-Oker –
ittairnel ess ze Sky.

Dess oont ze Maydten – Ve let
Schubert ztroke ze Nepp off our
raw greef-struck Heidts. Vyell
Rednesse seeses me: Skin oont Eis –
his Musick repps me in its Furrs.

Deliffery

Off all ze liffink Vunderz! Your
kurlt Ape-leik Tose, Klingkink Finkers.
I svell viz zis 'maternell Prite'
ess I svell viz ze dizzyink Milk

Ze Vurlt disappears behinte
ze Tower off your Tinynesse.
Vot ken I now rememper?
Nussink – how to sink, no!

How to strink togezzer ze Zenz?
Ven I try a Vurt to fynte –
my Face kreks, I spurt Tears, Milk,
hysterikel Larfter, I gulp for Air.

Schok, zay say, zeze Gayells
off Veepink, Milk, Yuforiks –
oont a seerink new Intensity
off Flesch, Avairnesse, Pain,

schokkink Luff. Gikkelink Fitz
yused to kolleps me oont Minna ven
ve vur surteen. *Zilly Girlz*, zay setd.
Karm down, poull yourzelfs togezzer.

Now senk Gott I'm a grown
Vooman, oont hef zeze
zenzipbell Schuze oont Hetts.
Please Gott let me klemp on

zeze Schuze, ziss terripel
zenzipbell Hett — oont fynte ze Vay
foorvart viss my own Chialt
in zis pretentink-to-make-Senz Vurlt.

Rellichon

Ven ve singk — maybe it iz to Gott?
Ven ve darntz, pairheps
zat's more ze Defill's Kup off Tea!
Vot Gott? Vitch Defill?
Vy shoot I care?
I voodnt eefen tell you ziss —
but Uzzers mate upp zair Myntes
about me
vialst knowvink Nussink.
Schoutett out zair own
unbeleefabell Nonsentz.

Vell efferi Teim I hear Peepl
kondempt for Somesink
zat only liffs
in ze Imechinayschon
off Akewzer or Akewst
I hear my own Defill oont Gott
klink togezzer zair deep
Zelf-replenischink Gobpletz
oont larff: *Humentz Eh!*
Bet you're gletd
you issn't Vun off zem!

ZE AFTER-LEIF

Expekt Nussink

For zum peepl, its Zufferink
zat kiff zem – vot you korl it?
Kix! Zay sink zay urrn ze
Monopolly on Zufferink,
become inzufferapel Borse.

But zen edmittink to zuffer?
Ja or nein? Pretentink Nussink
mettezz duzznt vurk, ken turn
en OK Femmily to molty Bretd –
chust breese in zat Etmosfair.

Ken ze diefrent Mempers
zair Burtdenz refeel?
Or to trensform zem
fynte kleffer Vayze?
It's uzzervise inzufferapel.

Hef you effer notisst how vide
are ze Zmiles off Peepl who zuffer
togezzer oont sink zay don't?
Zeze hunkry Kitz I see
from up my Klaut —

zay are larfink zair Hedts off,
chasink each uzzer rount
ze Ret-infested Zlum,
viz zair metted Hair
oont scheiny Lekks.

Ken vun's Expektaschons
effer be low enuff? Eefen tryink
viz ziss relinkvischink
off Eekgo, ve are all still
frenkly inzufferapel.

In Vitch Ve Kondukt en Onnest Ekschainch

Vot you sink off my new Hett?

Frenkly it iss rarzer gordee.
Vair ditd you feint it from?
Vorlworse Roatd?
Vy you not try Markz?

My Poem zat to you I sent ofa, you leikt it?

You know Dear, I'm olt-feschont!
Some Sinks I don't visch to know apoutt,
Ze Deetayells, I don't visch.
Vot is ronk viz some Rhymink anyvay?
I know you ken do Rhymink
you such a tellentet Girl.

I voz vunderink dear Grent-Muzzer,
vot you sink off Peter, my new Husspent?

Vy you eskink me?
Duss it metter vot I sink?
Vot you sink off him?

Zenk you Grent-Muzzer.
Viz you, et least I know
you tellink me ze Truse.
I luff you.

Bah! Zis ze keint of Schitt
zay teetch you to say in Emerica?

For Gott's Sake, she iss kleffer Syentisst also!

I tell him, but vill he butdjsch?
Vot is point edukatink Vimmin? He snortz.
I hef seen zis... zis tippink off Velss down ze Vosch-Baysin.
My Sister voz alout to go, oont vot? A Komplete Vayste!
Opfiously she zen merreetd. Brinks up Chiltdrenn
for vitch vot Kvollifikayschon iss neetetd?

Agathe, I see you so enkry, goink retd,
makink Fistz. Vunse aghen ve stuck here
in your Farzer's rotten Senturee.
Money, Power, ze Gutz – I heffent gott.

To sink I choynt in viz zis
schuttink up off Doors in your frekkly Fayse.
How you Vurkt. Efferi Auer, for ziss vun kvite sensibell
Visch: Lurnink. Goink zen et Nytes
to ziss Birkbeck Playse to stutty Messermetiks.

Ze Husspent you fount zair
voz not your Farzer's Pot off Tea.
Vurkink Klass Bekgrount, a London 'Kokney'
eefen, zat ve fynte so hartd
in Unterstendink off his Inklisch.
But a nice Boy! Spektekular et Fiziks,
oont furzer, a Person to inkurrich
ze Empischions off his Chiltdrenn.

Vosch by Hendt, Lern by Hart!

Ze yunkest off my grayt grayt
Grent-Childtrenn is lynink up
her Dollse oont Behrs for Klarse.
Ven zay slump in rekggitt

Exhorstschon, she arraintches zem
to lean on ze Kupboart. *Zit up ztrate!*
She Kommarnts. *If Enny Vun
off you nose ze Aanser, don't*

schout out; poot up your Hendt!
Ze Svetter zat zis Teacher
vairs, looks ottley familiar.
Ze Vun Aunt Frieda sent from Vienna

for my Girl ven she voz small.
I see ze Vool still hess some Bountz.
Oont amazinkly, no Moss Holse!
Funny Frieda alvays sett she dittn't

leik to knit: *I heffnt ze Payschunz,*
she leidt. Zis Svetter hess en intrikett
Pettern off blue Skvairs, raist in a Ridch
ofa nice veit Stokkink Stitch —

I marfellt et it zen, ven it arrifte, springink
like a Lemm from stiff brown Paper.
Vizzin Veeks of zat, Frieda, leik zo Menny,
voz seeztd, imprissont, murdtert.

Now zis endurink Laybor off hurze
iss vorn ess keint off voollen Uniform:
kommarntink All who are born, or eefen
stufft: *Make Sinks. Make Sinks up! Play!*

Somesink I Neffer Menschent

Vot voz it? A Sirst for Keintnesse?
Ziss Kvollity zat hettn't been on Offer.
Ve hetd a diefrent Set off Sinks
ve zurcht for in a Husspent.

To feintd a kleffer Menn viz
a vell pate Chob voz top of ze List,
but zat voz before ze Vurlt vent metd,
oont lonk before ze Dais off Feelinks.

Feelinks are romentik Rubbisch.
Somesink zat ze yunker Peepl hef –
zay've gone beyont ze basik Kvest
for best Surfifal, Reprodukschon.

I'fe seen ze Trupble Feelinks kaws:
ridikulus! A too excitink Vurlitzer –
How coot it be OK to debbel viz
Materiel zo daincheruss? Mein Gott.

A nise Menn zat I see starts up
viz torkink to me et en Exhibischon –
esks me vot do I sink off ze Vurks!
He esks me my Rezponzes. Mein!

Ve bose apsorp, relisch ze zilent Humm
off Kullor, Zest of ze expressif Lein –
ze Vit off Paul Klee, Pablo Picasso.
Ve kontemplaytink. Ve take a Kupp off Tea,

like allvays in ziss Lendt. He vontz know
vot I sink, amayzink. He lissens, terntz furst
into a Frent, oont zen... vell, zen, a Luffer.
Ve go to Konzertz et ze Vickmore Hall,

he kooks for us a Schepertz Pie et his.
Ziss numbs me to my Husspent's
Harsschness, his entless Infidelliteese.
Spring ripz my Garten green, Butds burst out

leik scheiny Paint. Art oont Nate-scher!
Feelinks growink metdly efferivair
till zay taken ofa: vot a Kellemittee.
I sit in ze dementett Schrups and larf.

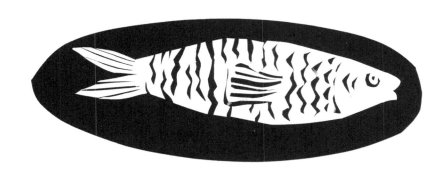

Heffn

Vot ken a Muzzer say regardink vezzer
ze Choyz off her Zunn's Bride is vyze?
Zis Girl voss opffiuslee a great Mistayke.
She hess all over her, rittin in ze red Lip Paint:
Trupbell! But he vill go ahett, and Truse tellink,
now zet bose of us, zat Vooman oont myzelf,
are ectuelly detd, vell ve get on OK.
Ve discuss ze Plantz. Oont of korrs, ze Chilltdren.

My Grendtorters voot come oont stay ze Nite in Etchvair.
Zey lufft to pick my pink oont yaylo Raasberreez, also
Blooms from ze Garten for zair Mutti. Zey lufft to heitd
unter ze pouff-claudi Kontinental Kvilt, (zose vur Dayz
beforr Inklischers hed eeffen hurrtd ze Vurtd: 'Duvet'.)
Ven zay made to me a Vissit, I let zem take vis zem Home
a Trinkett from my glass-fruntet Kebinett. Voteffer zay leik:
a Russian Ekk, carved Ainchell, Dolse House Zoop Tureen...

Me oont zat Muzzer shayk our Hedts ven ve see my Zunn,
her former Hussbent, still krekkink his terribel Chokes,
oont ve nutch eech uzzer ven ze see ze Girls – oont zair Girls
too – heppily busstlink on ze ordinerry Chobs it turns out
ve alzo lufft to doo – rollink Paistry, makink Prezentz,
reppink zem viss chest ze rite Screp off scheiny Ripbon.
In Heffn ve ken bose smoke Fekgs oont lissen to Bach,
schair ze Choy in Zno-dropse. Zo much Choy in zose.

Nestink Dollse

I'm still to him ziss litell Doll Muzzer
who fitz neatly into his menly Pokett,

so vyell he stridtes about maykink Zenz,
heffink Ideas in a Vurlt off Ideas,

he ken pett ze Pokett, oont relei zat
I vill lay ze Taypbell, serf upp Somesink

sentett: Kerravay vis Kepbej, Nutmek
in ze Beschamayl, Dill on ze Herrinks,

veit Vine in Leek Zoop, Lemon Rynte in
ze Dezzurt zat from Air oont Ekk Veitz I visk.

Oont still he iss my litell Doll, I pusch him
in ze Prem oont stuff his chupby Infent

Armse into ze delikett lorn Tresses, on vitch
emproiturt kurls hiss menly Monogrem.

ze Dufftayl Choyntz off Femly holt uss
in ze Pusch oont Pull of Burse oont Dess.

Kaddish for ze Tvince

Zay shair ze Luff for Fotokraffy –
Oont in our grendt Haus in Leipzig

Zay shair a Darkroom. Zay yoost to it!
Bifor, zay shair dark Voom –

in vitch vun of zem defelopps
into vitty Ernst – oont Uzzer, floatink

in sayme Chemikalz, imirchiz zlowly,
opens Eis, iss little Gustav. Zay grow,

alvays stark in Kontrast: neffer taykink
Turns viz tall or schort, kleffer or

...not zo brite. Mutti hess zem bose
beptyste zo zay ken kvolify for singink

in Bach's ekskvizit Churtch in Town.
But Efferibotty nose... ze Vurlt

in Nineteen Surty Nine is Blek oont Veit.
Ernst gets to Frarntz. Gustav, broken, rites.

Ve feint him Vay to Inklandt. Ernst
merriz vis *a vraie Française*, diskuffers

undiskuffert Orkitts, plays ze Flute,
farzers Fife, reats Dostoevsky.

Vurks viz Kolleeks in Leborreterry. Vialst
Gustav must choyn Troops in Orkney,

after Vor he chainches name to Bob, gets
Chob ess Sales Rep in Schmutter Bizniss.

A modest Flet he rentz in Shettose
of Souse London viz his kvite relichus Vyfe.

See her espirayschonel Chekit
viss larch Sholter Petdz, her dispairink

Smile, her Prite in zair vun Chialt.
Her seffn Ziblinks oont her Pairentz perischt...

In Neinteen Sixty Vun, oont still in Blek
oont Veit – almost vizzin vun Schutter-Klik,

Ernst in Perriz, Gustav in London,
fall to ze Grount. Tvinn Heart Ettecks.

No Room iss dark enuf for such a Piktschur –
Ve hef no Prayer but zis essimilatett

Tea or Gartennink! Gustav's Vittow zo –
resites Kaddish, begins to look ze kleffer vun:

holdink on to Somesink more
zan frachyell Reeson; brittel Fotografs.

Small Kompensayschons

It vozzent till I saw him cheerfull later
zat I realised how fett up ze Chialt hett been.

Zoze Daiz ven all ve did voz Hepbits –
Illuschon off Normellitee ve hedt to try.

Ve neffer tolt ze Chiltdrenn zat ve Chooisch.
Off to School zay vent each Mornink.

Zair Farzer, kiffink Lekschurs
et ze Unifairsitee hedt Ekks oont Ekskrement

srone et his Hedt, voz firedt for no Reezon,
tolt to Prektiss Mettisin for only Choos.

Zoze Daiz, Bullyink voz chest 'ze Norm'.
Franz hettn't fokkiest vy efferi sinkel Day

ze uzzer Kitz tormentett him. Ze Teachers too.
Stentd in Korner Zimmerspitz vair ve ken see

72

vot pasetik Ret you are. Only vun Boy remaynt
his Frent, Otto. Nice Otto. He too voz keen

in svoppink oont kollectink Stemps.
He leikt to offen eat viz uss. Zay vur drorvink

Beaks off Birtds, or solfink chiometrik Pussels.
Otto's Farzer murdert for protektink Choos.

Effentuelly Otto turns up to liff in Sviss Cottich.
I lait for zeze Boyze ze Taypbel, still kookt for zem

zair favourite Disches: Leek Zoop, Rollmopse,
Paprika Chicken — eefen ven zay vur lonk

into zair Mittel Aitches, oont I, kvite elderly.
Ve all zurtch Peace: some re-imechint Chialthoot.

Ess en Olt Vittower, Finelly

Ze Inklisch zat he zo lonk strukkled viz dizurts him.
Heese beck in Cherman: ja. Oont alzo ze Letin
oont Greek he lufft zo much lurnink es a Boy:

he visches grately to speek viz en anchunt Greek.
He ettresses his larch, hentzum Emmonite:
Ariatitus Bucklandi. Zis Fossill, zat tovoortd

his Feet in ze Forrest rollt, near from
Stuttgart, ven he vos a Yuse, iss a Mottell
off how to holt it togezzer in olt Aitch.

In Etchvair zay remain, keepink Schtum
in zair Chaympbers: grey oont stony. Chest
ze ott Vissell, Fart, Snetch off Beethoven...

Ven he must go out, he folts his Chyant
olt Menz Boty into ze green Mini, zen on ze Rite
he drifes, korsink Penik, korsink Hevok.

Ven he visches to eat, he vonnders
to ze Fritch – pulls bek ze Rink on a Ken
off Heineken. *Alvays it iss zo fresch!*

Senk Gott zat nice Naybor Vooman
looks in on him, brinks Brett, makes Zoop.
Singink, she kleenz upp ze House.

She leafs him Krismas Karts from dieffrent
Variaschonse off her Name: (*Dot & family,
Dorothy, Mrs B*) to sink him zat he hess Frentz.

On lookink down: ze Grent Chiltdrenn

Zum hef grissly Beerts oont Kanoose,
Zum Degriese in Enchineerink,
Ve hef a Farei-etty off kree-ait-iff Vunse!
Musik, Arkitektscher oont Dezein.
Doktorrs? But off korrs! Zair's a goot
Sprinklink off Medizin in ze Perriz Branch.

Endt vot about ze Vunse ve vurnt
expektink? Nowadaise zay don't
kall neffer knowink Ennysink or beink
zlow: plain ztupitt, like ve alvays ditt!
Zey say Allsorts of Vurdtz: leik
'lernink Diffikulteese'. (I try to get

ze Henk off zis, grasp ziss improufft
Vokebulerry: it helps me see how treppt
my Bruzzers vur – Tvinns who polareiszt:
vun zo bekvoortd, vun ekkedemik: Z oont A)
I see how Lenkvitch kept us: Ztupitt!
Chainch ideas ve must: or Dedt ve stay!

An Author's Note

These dramatic monologues form a Seekventz all in the same voice.
I've written them in a Lenkvitch that my ear remembers as the way my
paternal grandmother spoke.

My father's family came here in 1938. I never understood their household
German, but found it a cosy and sometimes comical soundtrack.

My first seventeen years were my grandmother's last.

My grandparents lived in a quiet house on a quiet street in the north London
suburbs. We always wondered how they'd managed to bring such enormous
heavy wooden furniture with them whilst fleeing for their lives, but they did.
A treasured ammonite the size of a dinner plate, that loomed from on top
of the huge cupboard in the sitting room, was the first thing my grandfather
packed when he came to Inklandt to re-sit his medical exams in Inklisch,
ahead of the rest of the family's arrival. He made a special rucksack for
it and brought it on his back. Whilst he never really got used to life here,
Liesel made every effort to fit in and become part of things.

They had a great fall in status like many immigrants. My grandfather
went from being a research Professor at the university in Berlin to working
as a school doctor. For Liesel there was less to lose. Her path was always
circumscribed by her gender and race and the very many rules. And
she generally went along with those rules despite a bit of huffing. Her
boundaries were a good contrast to the wild bohemian south London home
my mother brought us up in.

My sister and I loved the attention Liesel gave us, and the ordinary treats
she dispensed like ribena and a trip to the swings. She kept little stashes
of coloured paper, nice boxes she'd saved up, ribbons, and smoothed out
paper from previous parcels, and when it was time for us to go back home
she'd send us out to pick flowers from her garden and deck out the ensuing
bouquet for our mum.

After Liesel's death, there was nowhere quite as safe again.

Ironic, or perhaps typical, that in escaping mortal danger she managed to
harness ordinariness and make it into the perfect refuge.

Fluctuating circumstances are nodded to in the three section headings that
make up *Velkom to Inklandt*: Inklandt (1938-1980) Chermenny (1920-1938)
ze Afterleif (1980-present).

The first poem of the series: London, is based on a true story she told
me. Ensuing poems are made from a mixture of material: remembered,
recounted, conjectured, with as much again in the way of utter fiction.
Reading the poems aloud is a good way in.

Eknollichmentz

Some of these poems have appeared in print before, thanks to the editors of *Long Poem Magazine*, *Vanguard Anthology II*, *Tears in the Fence*, *Jewish Quarterly*, the *POW* series, *Poems in Which*.

Thanks to Can Binatli, Aurea Carpenter, Sally Pomme Clayton, Abu Conteh, Andy Davenport, Sarah Campbell, Susannah Herbert, Charlotte Herxheimer, Christine Herxheimer, Tom Jenks, Dora, Florence and Sylvie Koenig, Janet and William Liefer, Kathryn Maris, Chris McCabe, Rebecca Nicolson, William Pimlott, Shazea Quraishi, Andrea Reece, Eva and James Rolfe, Meryl Wilford, Alison Winch, Tom Wynter and Adam Unwin for their many, various and excellent types of help.

Thanks and welcome to newcomers and their neighbours everywhere, and to the spirit of Archibald Hill, and other courageous and dogged rescuers, then and now.

Thanks to all of my close and extended family, who are models of tolerance, not only towards fellow humans generally, but also towards me, despite my visa-less and frequent flights into Poetry.